lingvit‹

MY FIRST ITALIAN BOOK OF COLORS

ITALIAN-ENGLISH BOOK
FOR BILINGUAL CHILDREN

 www.lingvitokids.com

TROVALO, INDICALO E NOMINALO:
Find, point and name it:

1 **Membri della famiglia delle bacche**
Members of the berry family

2 **Creature del mare**
Creatures of the sea

3 **Ingredienti per cucinare**
Ingredients for cooking

4 **Frutti dolci**
Sweet fruits

5 **Oggetto a forma di triangolo**
Triangle shaped item

6 **Qualcosa di piccante e speziato**
Something hot and spicy

7 **Insetti che si posano sui fiori**
Insects that land on flowers

8 **Può essere visto in un giardino**
Can be seen in a garden

9 **Utilizzato dai vigili del fuoco per combattere il fuoco**
Used by firemen to fight fire

10 **Simbolo d'amore**
Symbol of love

Rosso
Red

il **lampone**
Raspberry

il **pomodoro**
Tomato

il **segnale di stop**
Stop sign

il **camion dei pompieri**
Firetruck

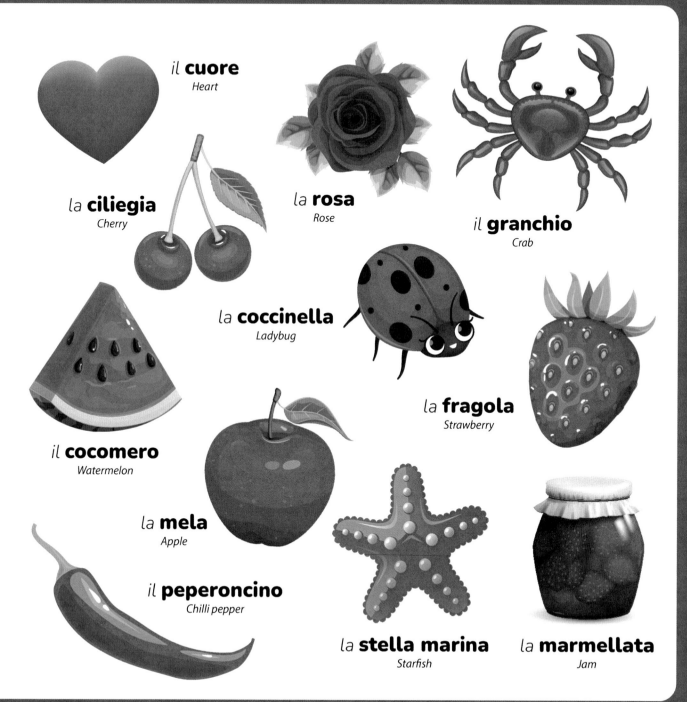

il **cuore**
Heart

la **ciliegia**
Cherry

la **rosa**
Rose

il **granchio**
Crab

la **coccinella**
Ladybug

la **fragola**
Strawberry

il **cocomero**
Watermelon

la **mela**
Apple

il **peperoncino**
Chilli pepper

la **stella marina**
Starfish

la **marmellata**
Jam

TROVALO, INDICALO E NOMINALO:

Find, point and name...

1 **Creatura lunga e strisciante**
Long and creeping creature

2 **Vivono sulla terra e nell'acqua**
They live on land and in water

3 **Insetto che può saltare alto**
Insect that can jump high

4 **Ingredienti nell'insalata**
Ingredients in a salad

5 **Può essere messo in un frullato**
Can be put in a smoothie

6 **Può essere visto su un albero**
Can be seen on a tree

7 **Verdura squisita**
Yummy vegetable

8 **Creature viscide**
Slimy creatures

9 **Può essere visto allo zoo**
Can be seen in a zoo

10 **Cresce dalla terra**
Grows from the ground

Verde
Green

la **cavalletta**
Grasshopper

la **pera**
Pear

il **serpente**
Snake

il **coccodrillo**
Crocodile

4

il **cetriolo**
Cucumber

la **foglia**
Leaf

il **kiwi**
Kiwi

l'**avocado**
Avocado

la **rana**
Frog

il **broccolo**
Broccoli

la **tartaruga**
Turtle

l'**erba**
Grass

5

TROVALO, INDICALO E NOMINALO:

Find, point and name...

1 **Creature con bellissime ali**
Creatures with beautiful wings

2 **Creature dell'oceano**
Creatures of the ocean

3 **Qualcosa che una persona può indossare**
Something a person can wear

4 **Frutta agrodolce**
Sweet and sour fruit

5 **Dove possiamo vedere grossi pesci**
Where we can see big fish

6 **Dove vediamo il sole e la luna**
Where we see the sun & moon

7 **Una cosa che mostra il tuo riflesso**
A thing that shows your reflection

8 **Dove le persone gettano immondizia**
Where people throw garbage

9 **Dove vediamo le barche**
Where we see boats

10 **Dove vediamo gli aeroplani**
Where we see airplanes

Blu
Blue

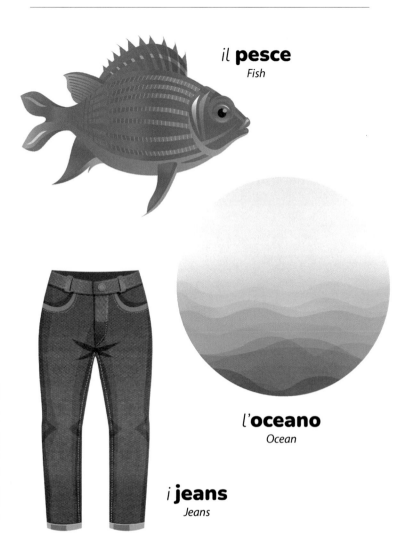

il **pesce**
Fish

l'**oceano**
Ocean

i **jeans**
Jeans

il **mirtillo**
Blueberry

la **ghiandaia azzurra**
Blue jay

il **cielo**
Sky

la **farfalla**
Butterfly

il **bidone dell'immondizia**
Trash can

lo **specchio**
Mirror

la **balena**
Whale

1 **Cose che possiamo vedere nel cielo**
Things we can see in the sky

2 **I frutti che possiamo vedere in una fattoria**
Fruits we can see in a farm

3 **Cibo che possiamo mangiare come spuntino**
Food we can eat as snack

4 **Creatura che fa il miele**
Creature that makes honey

5 **Cosa che fa dei suoni**
Thing that makes sounds

6 **Può essere indossato al dito**
Can be worn on the finger

7 **Può essere bevuto come succo**
Can be drank as juice

8 **Piccolo uccello con le ali**
Small bird with wings

9 **Cose che brillano**
Things that shine bright

10 **Colture che possono essere raccolte**
Crops that can be picked

Giallo

Yellow

la **pannocchia**
Corn

la **stella**
Star

l'**ape**
Bee

l'**anello**
Ring

il **sole**
Sun

il **limone**
Lemon

l'**ananas**
Pineapple

la **campana**
Bell

il **formaggio**
Cheese

il **pulcino**
Chick

il **pane**
Bread

le **patatine fritte**
French fries

TROVALO, INDICALO E NOMINALO:
Find, point and name...

1 **Animali con il becco**
Animals with beaks

2 **Cose che emettono suoni**
Things that make sounds

3 **Cose relative alle automobili**
Things related to cars

4 **Qualcosa che vedi a scuola**
Something you see in school

5 **Uccello che vive al freddo**
Bird that live in the cold

6 **Animali che vivono allo stato brado**
Animals that live in the wild

7 **Scudo per gli occhi**
Shield for the eyes

8 **Animale che corre veloce**
Animal that runs fast

9 **Uccelli che volano**
Birds that fly

10 **Animale che fa le ragnatele**
Animal that makes webs

Nero
Black

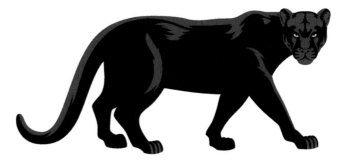

la **pantera**
Panther

gli **occhiali da sole**
Sunglasses

il **pinguino**
Penguin

il **ragno**
Spider

la **ruota**
Wheel

il **tucano**
Toucan

il **corvo**
Crow

il **pianoforte**
Piano

la **lavagna**
Blackboard

CIAO

la **strada**
Road

Bianco

White

TROVALO, INDICALO E NOMINALO:

Find, point and name...

1 Ingredienti per fare le frittelle
Ingredients to make pancakes

2 Qualcosa che vola nel cielo
Something that flies in the sky

3 Cose legate alla neve
Things related to snow

4 Usato per posizionare cibi e bevande
Used to place food and drinks

5 Usato per rendere le cose dolci
Used to make things sweet

6 Usato all'interno del bagno
Used inside the bathroom

7 Bevanda che viene dalle mucche
Drink that comes from cows

8 Qualcosa che ha un buon odore
Something that smells nice

9 Usato per fare il pane
Used to make bread

10 Animale che vive al freddo
Animal that lives in the cold

il **latte**
Milk

la **farina**
Flour

l'**aeroplano**
Airplane

il **riso**
Rice

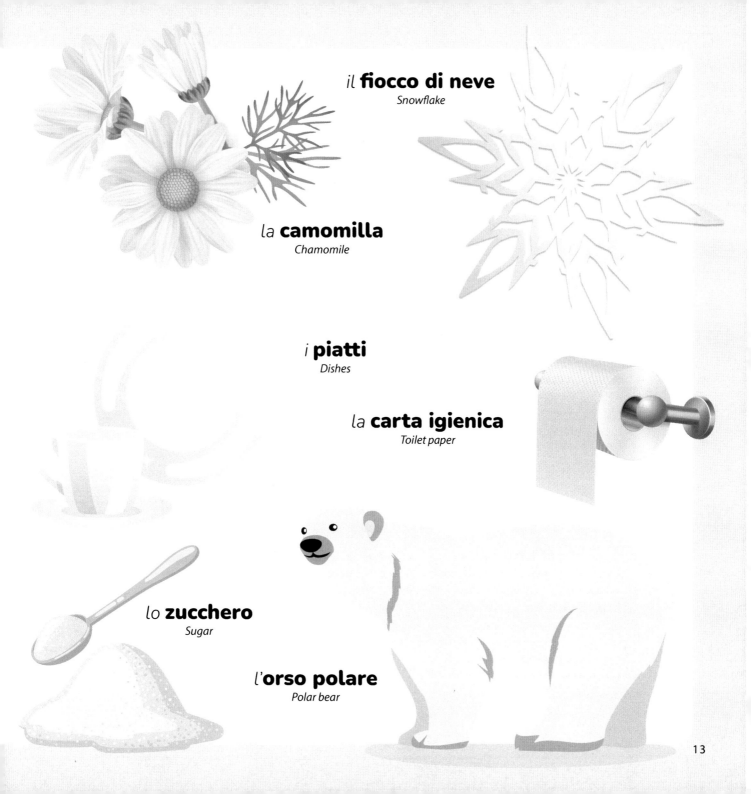

il **fiocco di neve**
Snowflake

la **camomilla**
Chamomile

i **piatti**
Dishes

la **carta igienica**
Toilet paper

lo **zucchero**
Sugar

l'**orso polare**
Polar bear

13

TROVALO, INDICALO E NOMINALO:
Find, point and name...

1 **Animali che corrono veloci**
Animals that run fast

2 **Animali nel mare**
Animals in the sea

3 **Animale che si arrampica sugli alberi**
Animal that climbs trees

4 **Usato come segnale di avvertimento**
Used as a warning sign

5 **Animali con code folte**
Animals with bushy tails

6 **Frutti che sono agrodolci**
Fruits that are sweet and sour

7 **La verdura preferita del coniglio**
Rabbit's favorite vegetable

8 **Cose con le strisce**
Things with stripes

9 **Cose che sono rotonde**
Things that are round

10 **Cose che sono a forma di triangolo**
Things that are triangle shaped

Arancione
Orange

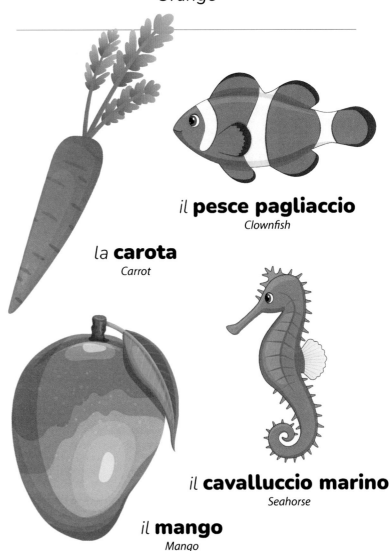

la **carota**
Carrot

il **pesce pagliaccio**
Clownfish

il **cavalluccio marino**
Seahorse

il **mango**
Mango

la **volpe**
Fox

l'**arancia**
Orange

la **tigre**
Tiger

il **cono stradale**
Traffic cone

la **foglia d'autunno**
Fall leaf

lo **scoiattolo**
Squirrel

la **zucca**
Pumpkin

TROVALO, INDICALO E NOMINALO:
Find, point and name...

1 **Cibo dolce**
Sweet food

2 **Piccole creature nell'oceano**
Small creatures in the ocean

3 **Animali che giocano nel fango**
Animals who play in mud

4 **Usato per colorare le labbra**
Used to color the lips

5 **Qualcosa che cresce dal suolo**
Something that grows from soil

6 **Parte del viso**
Part of the face

7 **Cose che hanno un buon odore**
Things that smell nice

8 **Uccello dalle gambe lunghe**
Bird with long legs

9 **Animale con i tentacoli**
Animal with tentacles

10 **Cibo freddo**
Food that is cold

Rosa
Pink

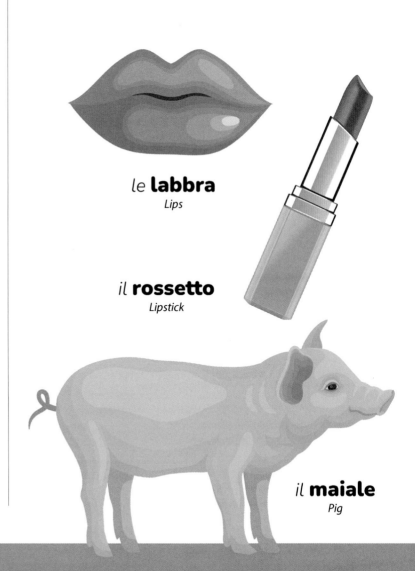

le **labbra**
Lips

il **rossetto**
Lipstick

il **maiale**
Pig

il **gamberetto**
Shrimp

le **peonie**
Peonies

la **ciambella**
Donut

il **ravanello**
Radish

la **medusa**
Jellyfish

il **fenicottero**
Flamingo

il **gelato**
Ice cream

il **verme**
Worm

TROVALO, INDICALO E NOMINALO:
Find, point and name...

1 **Frutta con i semi**
Fruits with seeds

2 **Creature del mare**
Creatures from the sea

3 **Cose profumate**
Things that are fragrant

4 **Frutti rotondi**
Fruits that are round

5 **Cose con i petali**
Things with petals

6 **Frutti che sono dolci**
Fruits that are sweet

7 **Frutta che può essere utilizzata come marmellata**
Fruits that can be used as jam

8 **Piante con le foglie**
Plants with leaves

9 **Cose che crescono sugli alberi**
Things that grow on trees

10 **Cose che sono lunghe**
Things that are long

Viola
Purple

la **melanzana**
Eggplant

il **lillà**
Lilac

la **prugna**
Plum

la viola
Pansy

l'**uva**
Grapes

il **guscio**
Shell

il **polpo**
Octopus

la **lavanda**
Lavender

il **fico**
Fig

Find, point and name...

Marrone

Brown

1 **Cose dolci**
Things that are sweet

2 **Animali che vivono allo stato brado**
Animals that live in the wild

3 **Cose con le punte**
Things with spikes

4 **Cose che cadono da un albero**
Things that fall from a tree

5 **Cose che puoi bere**
Things you can drink

6 **Cose che puoi mangiare**
Things you can eat

7 **Cose che puoi cuocere**
Things you can bake

8 **Uccello che non dorme di notte**
Bird that does not sleep at night

9 **Qualcosa che piace mangiare agli scoiattoli**
Something squirrels like to eat

10 **Qualcosa che cresce nei boschi**
Something that grows in woods

il **caffè**
Coffee

*l'*éclair
Eclair

la **patata**
Potato

il **fungo**
Mushroom

la **nocciola**
Nut

il **pane**
Bread

*l'***orso**
Bear

la **pigna**
Pinecone

il **gufo**
Owl

il **cioccolato**
Chocolate

il **cocco**
Coconut

il **riccio**
Hedgehog

TROVALO, INDICALO E NOMINALO:
Find, point and name...

1 **Oggetti appuntiti**
Pointed objects

2 **Qualcosa che scatta le foto**
Something that takes photos

3 **Animali a quattro zampe**
Animals with four legs

4 **Animali con le pinne**
Animals with fins

5 **Animali con le corna**
Animals with horns

6 **Creature oceaniche**
Ocean creatures

7 **Dove scorre l'acqua**
Where water flows

8 **Oggetti pesanti**
Heavy objects

9 **Oggetti in acciaio**
Objects made of steel

10 **Oggetto utilizzato sulla nave**
Object that is used on the ship

Grigio
Gray

la **forchetta**
Fork

il **topo**
Mouse

la **fotocamera**
Camera

l'**ancora**
Anchor

lo **squalo**
Shark

The Miraculous Journey Edward tulane

just any rabbit—he was made of the finest china and dressed in the most exquisite clothes. His owner, Abilene, adored him beyond measure. Every day, she would tell Edward how much she loved him, whispering it into his porcelain ears, brushing his fine clothes, and tucking him into bed at night. But Edward did not care. He cared only for his appearance and the admiration he received.Edward had no understanding of love. He spent his days gazing at his reflection in the mirror, admiring his dapper attire. To him, being loved seemed unnecessary. After all, why should he love others when he was so perfect on his own? He didn't even respond when Abilene would tell him how much he meant to her.Little did Edward know, his life was about to change in

Abilene was thrilled and, of course, brought Edward along. As they boarded the ship, Abilene cradled him in her arms, excited to show him the wonders of the sea. The ship was large and bustling, and Edward was content with his view of the waves from Abilene's arms, though he remained indifferent to her excitement.On the third day of the voyage, two mischievous boys noticed Edward sitting on a deck chair while Abilene was inside. They snatched him up and began tossing him between themselves. Edward was horrified but helpless, unable to move or speak. Suddenly, one of the boys threw Edward high into the air, and before anyone could stop him, Edward was flung over the side of the ship and into the cold, dark ocean.Edward plunged deep into the water, sinking further and further until he hit the ocean floor. Alone and forgotten, Edward's perfect clothes were ruined, and he was buried beneath the sand

darkness. He wondered if he would ever be found again, but he still didn't fully grasp what it meant to miss someone or to feel longing. He only knew that he was alone, and it was the first time he had ever felt the sting of being discarded.One day, after what seemed like an eternity, Edward was lifted from the water by a fisherman's net. The fisherman, Lawrence, looked at Edward curiously before bringing him home to his wife, Nellie. "Well, what do we have here? A fine rabbit, dressed up fancy," Lawrence said, handing Edward to his wife.Nellie smiled at the rabbit and decided to keep him. She cleaned Edward up and dressed him in baby clothes, calling him "Susanna." At first, Edward was appalled by his new appearance. He was no baby, and his fine suits were gone. However, Nellie was kind, and over time, Edward grew accustomed to his new life in the

care, placing him at the dinner Table, tucking him into bed, and talking to him as though he could understand. Though he still couldn't feel love, Edward started to sense that something about his life had changed. He wasn't admired for his appearance anymore, but for the company he provided.Then one day, everything changed again. Lawrence and Nellie's daughter, Lolly, came to visit. Unlike her parents, Lolly didn't care for Edward. She found him ridiculous, especially dressed in baby clothes, and without hesitation, she tossed Edward into the trash heap behind the house. Edward was once again discarded, buried beneath piles of garbage, feeling the crushing weight of abandonment.Lying in the dark, smelly heap, Edward's heart—if he had one—was heavy. He began to wonder why people discarded him so

remained buried beneath the refuse, forgotten once more. The loneliness was unbearable, but Edward had no choice but to endure it. He still couldn't comprehend why people seemed to discard him so easily. Was it something about him that made him unlovable?One day, a stray dog named Lucy came sniffing through the trash and found Edward. She gently pulled him out with her teeth, dragging him to her owner, Bull, a kind hobo who lived on the road. Bull smiled as he saw Edward. "Well, Malone, you're coming with us," he said, naming Edward after an old friend.Edward became a traveling companion to Bull and Lucy as they wandered from town to town, hopping on and off trains, and sleeping under the stars. Edward was no longer treated like a delicate china rabbit but as a simple companion, a fellow traveler. He learned what it meant to live without luxury, without the things that had once seemed so important.

outside of his own vanity. He listened as Bull spoke about the people they met, the hardships they faced, and the beauty of the simple moments they shared. Edward felt something stir deep inside him, something he hadn't felt before—a sense of connection to others, even if it was faint. But Edward's time with Bull and Lucy didn't last forever. One night, the police found Bull and Lucy sleeping by a campfire, and they forced them to leave the area. Bull had to move quickly, and in his haste, he left Edward behind. Once again, Edward was alone. This time, Edward was found by a young boy named Bryce, who lived with his sick sister, Sarah Ruth. Bryce took Edward home, and Sarah Ruth immediately fell in love with him. She cradled Edward as if he were the most precious thing in the world, her constant

much the little girl loved him, how she held him close when she coughed, how she whispered her thoughts and dreams to him late at night. Edward wanted, for the first time in his life, to comfort someone. He couldn't move or speak, but he wanted to offer more than just his presence.Sarah Ruth grew weaker with each passing day, and Edward remained by her side, helpless. Bryce, too, watched over his sister, but despite their care, Sarah Ruth's illness grew worse. One night, she passed away, leaving Bryce and Edward in quiet grief.Edward had never felt the sting of loss like this before. Sarah Ruth had loved him with all her heart, and now she was gone. Edward could do nothing but sit there, feeling the emptiness where Sarah Ruth's

city, looking for work. Times were hard, an
Bryce struggled to make enough money to
survive. He played the harmonica on street
corners, using Edward as a prop, but it
wasn't enough to get by. Eventually, Bryce
had no choice but to sell Edward to a
shopkeeper for a few dollars.Edward found
himself placed on a high shelf in a toy shop,
surrounded by other dolls and toys. Days
turned into weeks as he sat there, waiting
for someone to claim him. For the first time
in his life, Edward understood the pain of
being unwanted. He had experienced love and
loss, and now, he wondered if anyone would
ever love him again.As Edward sat in the
shop, he reflected on all the people he had
met—Abilene, Nellie, Bull, Lucy, Sarah Ruth.
He had been loved by so many, and yet he
had never truly understood the value of that
love until now. His heart, once cold and
unfeeling, had been changed by the journey
he had taken.

Edward sa. She pointed to him, her eyes wide with excitement. "Mommy, look! A rabbit!" she exclaimed. The girl's mother came closer, and when Edward saw her, his heart nearly stopped. It was Abilene, now grown up. Abilene picked Edward up gently, holding him in her hands as if she had found a long-lost treasure. She smiled, tears welling in her eyes. "I used to have a rabbit just like this," she whispered, remembering her childhood companion. The little girl, who was Abilene's daughter, hugged Edward tightly. "He's perfect," she said, beaming with joy. Edward felt a warmth he had never known before, a sense of belonging that filled his entire being. After all his travels, all his loss, Edward had finally

Maggie, was different from any he had experienced before. He no longer cared about his fine clothes or his perfect appearance. What mattered now was the love he felt in Maggie's arms, the way she cherished him just as Sarah Ruth and Abilene had.Edward had learned that love wasn't something that could be earned or demanded. It was a gift, something to be given and received without expectation. He had once been a proud, self-centered rabbit who thought only of himself, but

now, Edward understood that love was the most important thing in the world. It wasn't about being admired or kept in perfect condition; it was about being there for someone, even when times were hard, and even when you couldn't offer much in return.Maggie carried Edward everywhere, just like her mother had once done. Edward became her trusted companion through playtime and bedtime stories. And though Edward could never speak or move on his own, he felt connected to Maggie in a way he never had before. His heart, once cold and indifferent, was now filled with warmth and

He thought of all the people he had met, from Abilene to Lawrence and Nellie, from Bull and Lucy to Bryce and Sarah Ruth. Each of them had taught him something valuable about love, loss, and what it means to care for others. His life had been filled with heartbreak, but it had also been filled with love.He had learned that love sometimes meant enduring pain, that it sometimes meant saying goodbye. But even in the darkest moments, love was always there, waiting to be found again. Edward knew now that his journey hadn't just been about surviving—it had been about discovering what it truly meant

sat on the edge of her daughter's bed, looking down at the sleeping child and the rabbit beside her. Gently, she picked Edward up and held him close, her eyes soft with memories of the past. "Thank you," Abilene whispered, as if Edward could hear her. "Thank you for being there, for always coming back." Edward, resting in Abilene's hands, felt an overwhelming sense of peace. He had finally come full circle, back to the person who had loved him first. His journey had been long and full of unexpected turns, but it had brought him to a place of love, a place where he truly belonged. And so, in the quiet of the night, Edward Tulane, the once proud and heartless china rabbit, closed his eyes—not because he was tired, but because he was content. He had learned that life, with all its ups and downs, was a miraculous journey, and love was the greatest treasure

Made in the USA
Las Vegas, NV
29 November 2024

12895977R00017

l'elefante
Elephant

il rubinetto
Faucet

il koala
Koala

il coniglio
Rabbit

il procione
Raccoon

il pesce
Fish

il chiodo
Nail

la **pietra**
Stone

il **rinoceronte**
Rhinoceros

23

TROVALO, INDICALO E NOMINALO:
Find, point and name...

1 **Gli oggetti usati per realizzare l'arte**
Items used to make art

2 **Cose da trovare a scuola**
Things to find in school

3 **Animali colorati**
Colorful animals

4 **Cose che puoi vedere in cielo**
Things you can see in the sky

5 **FERMATI!/RALLENTA! VAI!**
STOP! SLOW DOWN! GO!

6 **Animali con le piume**
Animals with feathers

7 **Cose da vedere in un ristorante**
Things to see in a restaurant

8 **Qualcosa con cui giocano i bambini**
Where kids play

9 **Animali che possono cambiare colore**
Animal that can change color

10 **Cose con cui scrivere o disegnare**
Things to write or draw with

Multicolore
Multi color

l'arcobaleno
Rainbow

la **carta colorata**
Color paper

gli **anelli**
Stacking rings

l'hamburger
Hamburger

24

le matite colorate
Colored pencils

il pappagallo
Parrot

gli **acquarelli**
Paints

il **camaleonte**
Chameleon

la **mongolfiera**
Hot air balloon

il **parco giochi**
Playground

il **pavone**
Peacock

il **semaforo**
Traffic light

ITALIAN-ENGLISH BILINGUAL BOOKS SERIES

available at amazon

PART 2

MATCH COLORS

· ·

15
COLOR ACTIVITIES FOR KIDS

Collega i calzini abbinati
Connect the matching socks

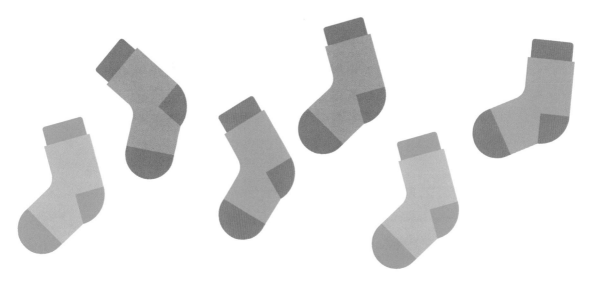

2

Trova le toppe abbinate ai vestiti
Find the matching patches for the clothes

Ordina i vestiti nelle scatole dello stesso colore

Sort clothing into boxes of the same color

Cerchia gli oggetti arancioni

Circle the orange items

Trova le toppe corrispondenti per ogni ombrello

Find the matching patches for each umbrella

Trova gli abiti abbinati ad ogni bambola

Find matching outfits for each doll

Collega ciascuna metà delle auto insieme

Connect each half of the cars together

Abbina ogni fiore a un vaso dello stesso colore

Match each flower to a vase of the same color

Abbina ogni matita al suo disegno colorato

Match each pencil to its colored drawing

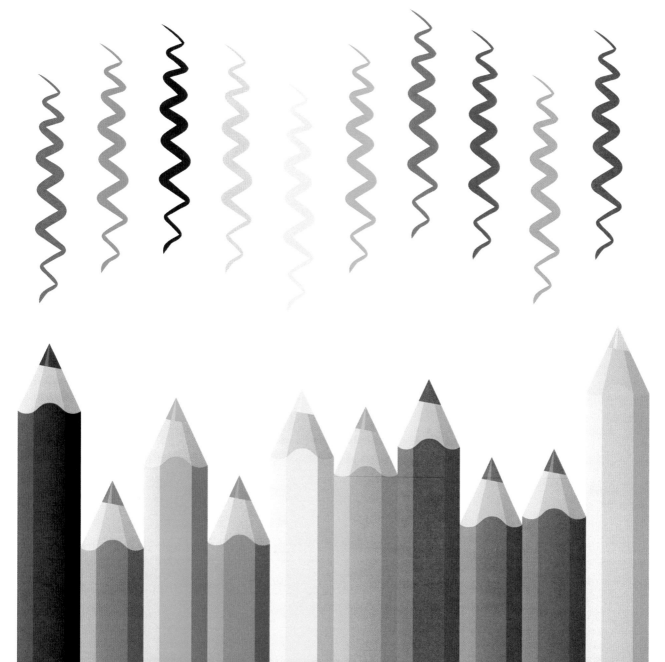

Abbina il gelato al cono per colore

Match the ice cream with the cone by color

Abbina ogni chiave con una serratura dello stesso colore

Match each key with a lock of the same color

Abbina il colore di questi oggetti
Match the color of these objects

Abbina il colore degli uccelli con quello delle loro casette
Match the color of the birds and their birdhouses

Abbina le farfalle con fiori dello stesso colore

Match the butterflies with flowers of the same color

Abbina ogni pallina con una combinazione di colori

Match each ball with a color scheme

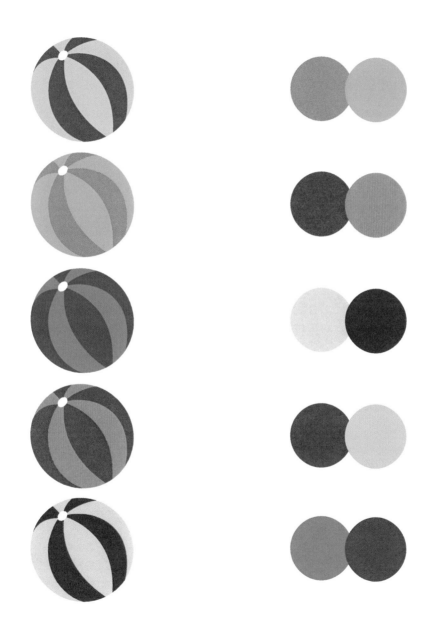

ITALIAN-ENGLISH BILINGUAL BOOK SERIES

lingvito books

26 Posts	266 Followers	248 Following

Lingvito Bilingual Books
📚 Educational books for bilingual children
✍️ Self-published author @annayoung1
🌍 40 plus languages 🪃
📖 Popularizing multi-language parenting 🌍✨
🔗 lingvitokids.com

Follow us
Instagram
@ingvito books

Available at **amazon**

Questions?
Email us at <u>hello@lingvitokids.com</u>

Made in the USA
Las Vegas, NV
29 November 2024

12895866R00026